Disney's
Winnie the Pooh
Everyone Is Special

Stripes or tails or feathers

Help make us

Who we are.

Be happy being

You each day,

And you'll bounce very far!

One lovely morning in the Hundred-Acre Wood, Tigger bounced over to Pooh's house for breakfast. When he arrived, Piglet and Pooh were sitting at the table eating.

"Good morning, Buddy Boys," Tigger called.

Tigger bounced right over to Pooh's mirror. He looked back and forth from the mirror to his friends.

"Just as I suspicionated," Tigger said thoughtfully. "No stripes."

"Whatever do you mean?" asked Piglet.

"You and Pooh don't have stripes!" Tigger insisted.

"Except on my shirt," Piglet replied, looking down.

"So why should I?" Tigger asked.

Pooh thought for a moment. "Because you're a tigger?" he said.

"That's no excuse!" Tigger sputtered.
And, in that very moment, Tigger decided that he would lose his stripes! The only question was…how?

"Why don't you talk to Kanga?" Piglet suggested. "She's very good at making chocolate and jelly disappear from Roo's shirts. Maybe she'll know how to make stripes go away."

So the three friends headed off to Kanga's house.
When Tigger told Kanga and Roo about his stripes, Kanga said, "I really like your stripes. Why do you want to lose them?"
"Without my stripes, I'll look more like everybody else!" Tigger replied.

Suddenly Roo had a great idea! He told Tigger to follow him into his room. There were little pots of paints everywhere. Roo, Piglet, and Pooh picked up paintbrushes and began to paint over Tigger's stripes.

By the time they were done, there was paint everywhere, but
no stripes to be seen. Tigger was a lovely orange color all over.
Kanga insisted that they all take a bath and clean up.

Tigger loved taking baths. He jumped right into the tub of soapy water. Soon the four friends stepped out and dried off.

"Why, Tigger," Roo giggled. "Your stripes are back."

"Imposterous!" cried Tigger, running to the mirror.

Tigger gasped when he saw his stripes. He was so sad, he didn't even feel like bouncing!

"Some nice dark mud might cover your stripes," Pooh said.

"That's it, Buddy Boy!" Tigger cried with joy. "I'll take a mud bath!"

Tigger bounced over to a nice muddy spot. He jumped right in and rolled around until he was covered in mud.

Eeyore happened to be strolling by when he saw Tigger knee-deep in mud.

"Missed a spot," Eeyore sighed, dipping his tail into the mud.

When they were finished, Tigger smiled. "Now, that should do the trick!"

"It'll do," Eeyore said. "But I thought the stripes were kinda nice."

But Tigger wasn't listening. He was too excited about
losing his stripes. "Race you to the bridge for a game of Pooh-
sticks!" he cried.

Everyone hurried off except for Tigger. He just stood there
covered in mud and as stiff as a statue.

Pooh turned around to see Tigger standing right where they
had left him. He hurried back to the mud puddle.

"This is ridickerous!" Tigger huffed. "If I can't move or
bounce, I won't feel like a tigger at all!"

Pooh, Piglet, and Eeyore carried Tigger to the stream and threw him in. When he was back to normal, Piglet asked him if he was ready to stop trying to lose his stripes.

"No sirree, Piglet ol' pal!" Tigger said. "Tiggers never give up!"

Pooh suggested that they visit his thoughtful spot to "think, think, think." He was sure that he could come up with an idea for losing Tigger's stripes.

"Hmmm," Pooh said thoughtfully. "I don't suppose you'd like to try my special honey dip."

"I'll try anything to lose these stripes, Buddy Boy," Tigger said, perking up. "Er, what is a honey dip?"

They all went back to Pooh's house and gathered several honey pots. Then Pooh took Tigger outside and poured honey all over him.

The thick, gooey honey had covered Tigger's stripes completely. Now Tigger was a lovely golden color.

But no sooner were they done, when a swarm of bees flew by and chased Tigger back to the bridge.

Tigger took a deep breath and jumped into the stream. He had been through a painting party, a mud bath and a "honey dip." What else was a tigger to do?

Looking up, Tigger saw Owl flying overhead.

"Halloo, Tigger!" cried Owl. "I could see those big, bold stripes of yours a mile away!"

Suddenly Tigger felt very proud.

On his way back to Pooh's house, Tigger bounced by Rabbit's. "Glad you stopped by," said Rabbit. "I wanted you to see my striped tulips. I got the idea to plant them from your stripes!"

Tigger began to think. Hadn't everyone said that they really liked his stripes? Why, his stripes had even helped Owl spot him from way up high! Now they'd given Rabbit the idea for a new flower! Imagine that!

"Hoo-hoo-hoo!" Tigger chuckled. "Stripes are splendiferous!"

And feeling like his old, bouncy self, Tigger bounced back to
Pooh's to make an announcement.

"I've made up my mind, Buddy Boys," Tigger said. "I've decided
to keep my stripes! Why, I just wouldn't be me without them."

After all, that's what makes me special!

A LESSON A DAY
POOH'S WAY

Everyone is special

in his own way—

especially tiggers!